HOME MAINTENANCE LOG FOR

ADDRESS

_____

_____

_____

DATE OF PURCHASE

_____

Systems Maintenance By Month

JANUARY
Clean Pipes (Descale overnight)
Clean Showerheads and Taps
Clean and Recaulk Shower/Sinks
Clear Ice Dams In Gutters

FEBRUARY
Deep Clean Oven and Stovetop
Clean Washer
Clean Dyer and Check Vent
Clean Dishwasher & Check Filter

MARCH
Deep Spring Clean
Check Roof for Soft Spots
Check Sump Pump
Clean Gutters

Systems Maintenance By Month

APRIL
Spring Clean Kitchen
Vacuum HVAC Unit
Inspect Attic
Have AC Tuned

MAY
Check Exhaust Fans
Check Ceiling Fan Blades/Dust
Check Weather Stripping
Fix Rust Spots

JUNE
Clean Window Wells
Remove Dead Limbs From Trees
Touchup Paint
Remove Dead Plants From Flowerbeds

Systems Maintenance By Month

JULY
Clean/Stain Deck
Maintain Garage Door
Power Wash Concrete
Check Ductwork for Leaks

AUGUST
Clean Garbage Disposal
Clean Out Freezer
Clean Window Treatments
Change Air Filters

SEPTEMBER
Flush Water Heater
Furnace Tune-Up
Check Pantry for Expired Food
Check Carbon Monoxide Detectors

Systems Maintenance By Month

OCTOBER
Remove Exterior Hoses & Drain
Vacuum & Clean Furnace
Deep Clean Microwave
Winterize AC

NOVEMBER
Vacuum Fridge Coils
Deep Clean Fridge
Clean Fridge Drain Pan
Clean Circuit Breakers

DECEMBER
Test Electrical Outlets
Run Water in Unused Rooms
Inspect Fire Extinguishers
Replace Smoke Detector Batteries

Repairman Contact Information

Company Name:_____
Phone Number:_____
Email:_____
Technician Name:_____

Company Name:_____
Phone Number:_____
Email:_____
Technician Name:_____

Company Name:_____
Phone Number:_____
Email:_____
Technician Name:_____

Company Name:_____
Phone Number:_____
Email:_____
Technician Name:_____

Repairman Contact Information

Company Name:_____
Phone Number:_____
Email:_____
Technician Name:_____

Company Name:_____
Phone Number:_____
Email:_____
Technician Name:_____

Company Name:_____
Phone Number:_____
Email:_____
Technician Name:_____

Company Name:_____
Phone Number:_____
Email:_____
Technician Name:_____

Repairman Contact Information

Company Name:_____
Phone Number:_____
Email:_____
Technician Name:_____

Company Name:_____
Phone Number:_____
Email:_____
Technician Name:_____

Company Name:_____
Phone Number:_____
Email:_____
Technician Name:_____

Company Name:_____
Phone Number:_____
Email:_____
Technician Name:_____

Home Warranty Information:

Company:_____

Premium Paid:_____

Contract Length:_____

Policy Number:_____

Customer Service Number:_____

Online Login User Name:_____

Online Login Password:_____

Appliances Covered:

	Refrigerator			Ice Maker
	Stove			Garbage Disposal
	Washer			Other
	Dryer			Other
	Dishwasher			Other
	Built-In Microwave			Other
	Trash Compactor			Other

Home Warranty Information (Continued):

Systems Covered:

Air Conditioning	
Heating	
Electrical	
Door Bell	
Smoke Detectors	
Ceiling Fans	
Water Heater	

Central Vac.	
Septic Pump	
Well Pump	
Other	
Other	
Other	
Other	

Usage Log:

Date	What Was Serviced	Problem	Service Technician

Home Warranty Information (Continued):

Date	What Was Serviced	Problem	Service Technician

Appliance Information

Date of Purchase	Appliance	Purchased From	Price	Serial Number	Warranty

Appliance Information

Date of Purchase	Appliance	Purchased From	Price	Serial Number	Warranty

Appliance Information

Date of Purchase	Appliance	Purchased From	Price	Serial Number	Warranty

Appliance Repair Log

Date of Service	Appliance	Repairman	Contact Info	Cost	Warranty

Appliance Repair Log

Date of Service	Appliance	Repairman	Contact Info	Cost	Warranty

Appliance Repair Log

Date of Service	Appliance	Repairman	Contact Info	Cost	Warranty

Monthly Maintenance Log

Date	Check Smoke Detectors	Change Furnace Filter	Other:	Other:	Performed By (Initials)

Monthly Maintenance Log

Date	Check Smoke Detectors	Change Furnace Filter	Other:	Other:	Performed By (Initials)

Monthly Maintenance Log

Date	Check Smoke Detectors	Change Furnace Filter	Other:	Other:	Performed By (Initials)

Quarterly Maintenance Log

Date	Check Basement/Crawl Space For Leaks	Clean Fridge	Clean Baseboards	Check Shower/Sink Drain Issues	Performed By (Initials)

Quarterly Maintenance Log

Date	Check Basement/Crawl Space For Leaks	Clean Fridge	Clean Baseboards	Check Shower/Sink Drain Issues	Performed By (Initials)

Quarterly Maintenance Log

Date	Check Basement/Crawl Space For Leaks	Clean Fridge	Clean Baseboards	Check Shower/Sink Drain Issues	Performed By (Initials)

Yearly Maintenance Log

Date	Smoke Detector Batteries	Carbon Monoxide Detector	Clean Gutters	Other:	Other:	Performed By (Initials)

Yearly Maintenance Log

Date	Smoke Detector Batteries	Carbon Monoxide Detector	Clean Gutters	Other:	Other:	Performed By (Initials)

Yearly Maintenance Log

Date	Smoke Detector Batteries	Carbon Monoxide Detector	Clean Gutters	Other:	Other:	Performed By (Initials)

Notes

Notes

Notes

Notes

Notes

Notes

Notes

Notes

Notes

Notes

Notes

Notes

Notes

Notes

Notes

Notes

Notes

Notes

Notes

Notes

Notes

Notes

Notes

Notes

Notes

Notes

Notes

Notes

Notes

Notes

Notes

Notes

Notes

Notes

Notes

Notes

Notes

Notes

Notes

Notes

Notes

Notes

Notes

Notes

Notes

Notes

Notes

Notes

Notes

Notes

Notes

Notes

Notes

Notes

Notes

Notes

Notes

Notes

Notes

Notes

Notes

Notes

Notes

Notes

Notes

Notes

Notes

Notes

Notes

Notes

Notes

Notes

Notes

Notes

Notes

Notes

Notes

Notes

Notes

Notes

Notes

Notes

Notes

Notes

Made in United States
Orlando, FL
05 August 2022

20551275R00065